Costa Rica
ABCs

A Book About the People and Places of Costa Rica

by Sharon Katz Cooper   illustrated by Allan Eitzen

Special thanks to our advisers for their expertise:

Jill Calderón, Program Director
Latin America Center for Latin American Studies
and the Office of Study Abroad and Student Exchange
University of Arizona

Susan Kesselring, M.A., Literacy Educator
Rosemount–Apple Valley–Eagan (Minnesota) School District

PICTURE WINDOW BOOKS
Minneapolis, Minnesota

Editor: Jill Kalz

Designers: Joe Anderson and Abbey Fitzgerald

Page Production: Angela Kilmer

Art Director: Nathan Gassman

Associate Managing Editor: Christianne Jones

The illustrations in this book were created with acrylics.

Picture Window Books

5115 Excelsior Boulevard

Suite 232

Minneapolis, MN 55416

877-845-8392

www.picturewindowbooks.com

Printed in the United States of America.

Library of Congress Cataloging-in-Publication Data

Cooper, Sharon Katz.

Costa Rica ABCs : a book about the people and places of Costa Rica /

by Sharon Katz Cooper ; illustrated by Allan Eitzen.

p. cm. — (Country ABCs)

Includes bibliographical references and index.

ISBN-13: 978-1-4048-2249-8 (library binding)

ISBN-10: 1-4048-2249-6 (library binding)

1. Costa Rica—Juvenile literature. 2. Alphabet books. I. Eitzen, Allan. II. Title.

F1543.2.C66 2006

972.86—dc22

2006027230

¿Cómo está usted?
(KOH-moh eh-STAH oo-STEHD)

That means "How are you?" in Spanish, the official language of Costa Rica. Costa Rica is a country in Central America. It is small in size but rich in culture and natural beauty. *Costa Rica* means "rich coast."

Nicaragua

Caribbean Sea

COSTA RICA

San José

Pacific Ocean

Panama

FAST FACT:
Costa Rica's population is about 4 million.

A is for art.

Carving is the oldest art form in Costa Rica. Carved objects made of jade (a green stone), gold, and clay are common throughout the country. Many artists sell handmade wooden furniture, carved bowls, and jewelry to tourists as souvenirs.

B is for Bribri (BREE-BREE).

The Bribri are one of the Native American groups who live in Costa Rica. Some of them live on a reservation in the southeastern part of the country. Many Bribri live in simple homes made of palm leaves and bamboo.

FAST FACT:
The Bribri make their living as farmers. They raise more than 100 species of crops for food, building materials, medicine, crafts, firewood, and trade.

C is for coffee.

Costa Rica was the first country in Central America to grow coffee beans. Coffee has been a big part of the country's economy since the early 1800s, and it is now Costa Rica's most important export.

FAST FACT:
Costa Ricans grow coffee beans on more than 100,000 small and large farms throughout the country.

D is for democracy.

Costa Rica's system of government is a democracy. It is similar to the United States government, with a president, a house of representatives, and courts. Costa Rica has been a very stable and peaceful country under its democratic system.

FAST FACT:

All Costa Ricans over age 18 have the right to vote. Costa Rica held its first presidential election in 1890—the first democratic election in Central America.

E is for ecotourism.

Ecotourism means visiting places without disturbing the natural landscape or the plants and animals that live there. Many ecotourists travel to Costa Rica every year. They visit the country's beautiful rain forests and explore its coastlines.

FAST FACT:
Almost 1 million tourists visit Costa Rica each year.

F is for flag.

Costa Rica's flag is blue, white, and red. The blue stripes stand for the sky and the ocean. The white stripes stand for peace. The red stripe in the middle stands for the blood shed by Costa Rica's national heroes.

G is for gallo pinto (GAH-oh PEEN-toh).

Gallo pinto is the official meal of Costa Rica. It is a food made from black beans, white rice, onions, peppers, and spices. It is sometimes served with scrambled eggs. Costa Ricans often eat *gallo pinto* for breakfast.

FAST FACT:
Gallo pinto means "spotted rooster" in Spanish.

H is for hydroelectricity.

When water flows through a hydroelectric dam, it helps create electricity. Costa Rica has a dozen large hydroelectric power plants on its rivers. These power plants provide the country with almost all of the electricity it needs.

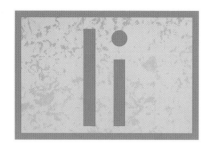

I is for insect.

More than 35,000 species of insects live in Costa Rica's many rain forests and national parks. Ten percent of the world's butterflies are found there, as well as thousands of different kinds of beetles, moths, grasshoppers, and ants.

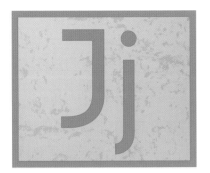

J is for Juan Santamaría.

Juan Santamaría is one of Costa Rica's national heroes. In 1856, an outside army tried to take over Costa Rica. The Costa Ricans chased the army into Nicaragua, where the invaders hid in a wooden fort. As the legend goes, Juan Santamaría ran into the fort with a torch and burned the fort down. The victory helped Costa Rica maintain its freedom.

FAST FACT:
Costa Ricans celebrate Juan Santamaría Day on April 11 every year.

K is for kingfisher.

Kingfishers are colorful birds that are common in Costa Rica. Six different kinds of kingfishers live in Costa Rica. They are among almost 850 species of birds in this small country.

FAST FACT:

Costa Rica has more species of birds than either North America or Europe.

L is for Limón.

Limón is the Caribbean coastal region of Costa Rica. It is also the name of the country's most important port city. Most of Costa Rica's exports are sent by ship from Limón to countries around the world.

FAST FACT:
Explorer Christopher Columbus dropped his anchor near present-day Limón in 1502, during his final sea voyage to the New World.

15

M is for Monteverde.

Monteverde Cloud Forest Reserve is Costa Rica's most visited natural area. This reserve is called a cloud forest because the trees are almost always covered in mist. The park is home to more than 400 species of birds, 5,000 species of moths, 100 species of mammals, and more than 2,000 kinds of plants.

N is for national parks.

National parks make up about 25 percent of Costa Rica. These protected lands cannot be disturbed by logging or farming. Within the national rain forests, wetlands, and beaches live thousands of species of animals, including giant anteaters, macaws, and sloths.

FAST FACT:
In spring and summer, many people travel to Tortuguero National Park to see four kinds of rare sea turtles lay their eggs on the beach.

O is for oxcart.

Brightly colored oxcarts are the national symbol of Costa Rica. Once used to bring fruits and vegetables to markets, today the carts can be seen at festivals. The artists of Sarchí, a small town in the heart of Costa Rica, are well known for their beautiful, hand-painted oxcarts.

FAST FACT:
No two oxcarts are painted exactly the same. Each has its own unique design.

18

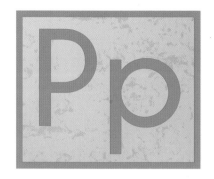

P is for Punto Guanacasteco
(POON-toh gwahn-ah-cah-STEH-koh).

When the sounds of guitars and marimbas fill the air, Costa Rican couples may be doing the *Punto Guanacasteco*. This traditional dance comes from the Guanacaste province in northwestern Costa Rica. Women often wear brightly colored skirts designed to look like the wheels of decorated oxcarts.

19

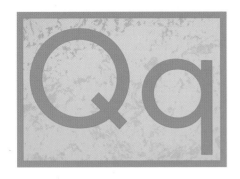

Q is for quetzal.

The quetzal is a colorful bird found in Costa Rica's cool, mountain forests. The male has long, flowing green tail feathers, which ancient peoples used in ceremonies and on headdresses. The quetzal was worshipped as a god of the air.

FAST FACT:
Today, the quetzal is quite rare, partly because its habitat is threatened in many places by logging and farming.

R is for rain forests.

Costa Rica is rich in rain forests, which are home to some of the greatest numbers of plants and animals in the world. In some of Costa Rica's rain forests, more than 240 inches (610 centimeters) of rain fall each year.

S is for Óscar Arias Sánchez.

Óscar Arias Sánchez was the president of Costa Rica from 1986 until 1990. While he was president, Sánchez won the Nobel Peace Prize for his work in bringing peace to the Central American region. He was re-elected president in 2006.

FAST FACT:
Sánchez used his Nobel Peace Prize money to establish the Arias Foundation for Peace and Human Progress.

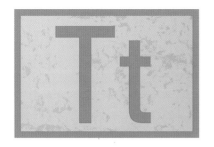

T is for Ticos (TEE-kohs).

Costa Ricans call themselves *Ticos*, a nickname that comes from the phrase "We are all *hermaniticos* (little brothers)." The nickname is meant to show that all people are equal.

FAST FACT:
If someone from Costa Rica wants to describe something as very Costa Rican, he might say, "*Es muy tico*," which means, "It is very *Tico*."

23

U is for University of Peace.

Unlike many of its neighboring countries, Costa Rica has been stable and peaceful for a very long time. As a result, the United Nations chose Costa Rica as the site of the University of Peace. Students there can take classes in human rights, saving energy, living peacefully, and improving the environment.

FAST FACT:
Costa Rica abolished, or ended, its army in 1949.

V is for volcanoes.

Costa Rica is located along the "Ring of Fire," a circle of volcanoes that surrounds the Pacific Ocean. One of the country's most active volcanoes is Arenal, which towers over the eastern shore of Lake Arenal. Some days, Arenal erupts every 30 minutes or so.

W is for white-water rafting.

Rivers flowing from the mountains to the oceans provide great spots for white-water rafting in Costa Rica. Two of the best-known white-water rivers are the Río Reventazón and the Río Pacuare. The Río Pacuare is considered one of the top 10 rivers in the world by many rafters and kayakers.

X is for exports.

Costa Rica's most important exports are coffee, bananas, and sugar. The country also exports pineapples, cotton, electronics, medical equipment, flowers, vegetable oils, and cocoa beans.

FAST FACT:
Almost half of Costa Rica's exports are sold to the United States.

Y is for yuca (YOO-kah).

Yuca is a potato-like vegetable used in Costa Rican cooking. It has a buttery flavor. Yuca can be used to make french fries, pancakes, and pudding.

Z is for Zoo Ave.

Zoo Ave is a zoo in the central valley of Costa Rica. It is dedicated to education, respect for local animals, and the breeding of endangered species. The zoo houses the largest bird collection in Central America, with more than 100 different species. In Spanish, *Ave* (AH-veh) means "bird."

FAST FACT:
Zoo Ave is one of only two zoos in the world that houses quetzals, the rare birds found in Costa Rica's mountain forests.

29

Costa Rica in Brief

Official name: Republic of Costa Rica

Capital: San José

Official language: Spanish

Population: about 4 million

People: 94 percent European origin (Spanish), 3 percent black, 1 percent Native American, 1 percent Chinese, 1 percent other

Religions: mostly Roman Catholic, with small groups of Protestants

Education: free and mandatory from age 6 to 15

Major holidays: New Year's Day (January 1), Easter (March/April), Juan Santamaría Day (April 11), Guanacaste Day (July 25), Independence Day (September 15), Christmas Day (December 25)

Transportation: trains, cars, boats

Climate: tropical and subtropical; cooler in highlands; dry season from December to April, rainy season from May to November

Area: 19,730 square miles (51,100 square kilometers)

Highest point: Cerro Chirripó, 12,573 feet (3,810 meters)

Lowest point: sea level

Type of government: democracy

Most powerful government official: president

Major industries: microprocessors, food processing, textiles and clothing, construction materials, fertilizer, plastic products

Natural resources: hydroelectricity

Major agricultural products: coffee, pineapples, bananas, sugar, corn, rice, beans, potatoes, beef, timber

Chief exports: coffee, bananas, sugar, pineapples, textiles, electronics, medical equipment

National symbol: oxcart

Money: Costa Rican colón

Say It in SPANISH

hello.	*hola* (OH-lah)
goodbye.	*adios* (ah-dee-OHS)
thank you	*gracias* (GRAH-see-ahs)
please.	*por favor* (POR fah-VOHR)
one	*uno* (OO-noh)
two	*dos* (DOHS)
three	*tres* (TREHS)
yes	*sí* (SEE)
no	*no* (NOH)

Glossary

culture—the shared beliefs and customs of a particular group of people

democracy—a kind of government in which the people make decisions by voting

economy—a country's trade in products, services, and money

endangered—when an animal is one of the few of its kind left in the world

habitat—the place where an animal or plant lives

hydroelectric—making electric power from the force of moving water

legend—a story that may not be all true but may have some true parts

marimbas—xylophone-like instruments

province—a division within a country

reserve—land used for a special purpose

species—groups of animals or plants that have many things in common

To Learn More

At the Library

Deady, Kathleen W. *Costa Rica*. New York: Children's Press, 2004.

Englar, Mary. *Costa Rica: A Question and Answer Book*. Mankato, Minn.: Capstone Press, 2006.

Fox, Mary Virginia. *Costa Rica*. Chicago: Heinemann, 2001.

Garrett, Rosalie. *Welcome to Costa Rica*. Milwaukee: Gareth Stevens, 2001.

On the Web

FactHound offers a safe, fun way to find Web sites related to this book. All of the sites on FactHound have been researched by our staff.

1. Visit *www.facthound.com*

2. Type in this special code: 1404822496

3. Click on the FETCH IT button.

Your trusty FactHound will fetch the best sites for you!

Index

Look for all of the books in the Country ABCs series:

Australia ABCs
Brazil ABCs
Canada ABCs
China ABCs
Costa Rica ABCs
Egypt ABCs
France ABCs
Germany ABCs
Guatemala ABCs
India ABCs

Israel ABCs
Italy ABCs
Japan ABCs
Kenya ABCs
Mexico ABCs
New Zealand ABCs
Russia ABCs
The United States ABCs
Venezuela ABCs
Vietnam ABCs